TOTALLY U*NIQUE* THOUGHTS

Reminders of Life's Everyday Magic

Michael Dooley

Published by
Totally Unique Thoughts®

©1998 by TUT Enterprises, Inc.
Published by Totally Unique Thoughts®
    a Division of TUT® Enterprises, Inc.
    Orlando, Florida * http://www.tut.com
Printed in Canada on acid free-paper.
Cover photo copyright © 2005 Monique DiCarlo,
monique.dicarlo@gmail.com
Cover and book designs by Andy Dooley,
www.andydooley.com
All "thoughts" by Michael Dooley, except
page 131, co-written with Andrew Dooley,
pages 15, 19, 22, 90, 106, 118, 120, 121, 123 by
Andrew Dooley, and pages 93, 98, 115, 123
by Sheelagh Mawe. Amanda girl, we love
you!
All rights reserved. No part of this book
may be reproduced, stored or transmitted
in any way of form without written permis-
sion from the publisher, except by a re-
viewer who may quote brief passages in a
review or article.
Library of Congress Catalog
Card Number: 98-96084
10 Digit ISBN 0-9642168-1-7
13 Digit ISBN 978-0-9642168-1-7

To the
Totally Unique Thinker
in you.

FOREWORD

Almost 10 years ago, an artist, a CPA, and their cool mom got together and launched TUT, a company that would sell "Totally Unique T-shirts".

It was painfully slow-going in the beginning, but eventually we grew from retailing out of a pushcart into our own stores, and from wholesaling locally to wholesaling internationally.

From the start, what made us "Totally Unique" was our style of graphics, but somewhere along the way we began adding our thoughts about life, dreams and happiness to the designs. Not that we're experts or anything, but these are the things that we think about more often than not, and at some point they kind of spilled over onto the T-shirts.

Lately, with these thoughts becoming such a "thing" for us, we're now getting almost as many requests for a book of them, as we're being told that not everyone likes having the front of their T-shirt read! So for those of you who are a bit shy, and for the show-offs too, we've put together this collection of our most "Totally Unique Thoughts" so far, sort of like... TUT Unplugged.

June 1998

TOTALLY

U
N
I
Q
U
E

THOUGHTS

Reminders of Life's
Everyday Magic

Far out in the ocean
On a moonlit night,
A circle of dolphins
Slips out of sight.
They're on a mission
Of the grandest scale,
To spread the word
To every minnow and whale:
That life's an illusion
Just waiting for you -
To believe in your dreams
So that they can come true!

A flower is simple
Its message is true,
The earth is happy
There are people like you.

An infinite drop
In an infinite sea,
Like an infinite you
And an infinite me.

Picture in your mind
All that you may be,
And with a little time
You will come to see:
That in the game of life
Your dreams will come alive,
By thinking of the end result
As if it had arrived!

Do what you love,
Love what you do,
And the world
Will come
To you!

When our hands
Are joined together,
Peace and love
Will reign forever.

In the jungle there's a secret
That all the animals keep,
And in the ocean it's no different,
Their code runs just as deep:
Whether the hunter or the hunted,
Your fate is just as grand,
Because in the final hour
You'll meet again as planned.
For neither is the victor
They just fulfill the plan,
And the same is true of people -
Each does the best they can.

The fish in the sea
Swim from shore to shore,
Searching for meaning
On the ocean floor.
And we are the same
In time and space,
Though what we need most,
Comes not from a place.

Walk in the green forest of silence,
Swim in the blue ocean of Joy,
Dance in the golden light of Love,
And laugh in the raging river of Life.

The weather may storm
And the bow may break,
On the quest for treasure
We all must make.
But when the chest is found
And the gold revealed,
The secret of life
Remains concealed.
Because the truth that we seek
Lies not in the sand,
But in the hearts and souls
Of every woman and man.

Like the sun in the morning
You brighten my day,
And like the stars at night
You show me the way.

If you find money spend it.
If you're given love, give it back.
And if the power of life calls,
ANSWER.

Your dreams are gifts
That set you in motion,
On the tides of time
Where life is an ocean.
And your sails are filled
With the winds of desire,
To surge through the waves
Of murk and mire.
But when you awaken
With your goal at hand,
You'll see your true destination
Was the voyage, not the land.

Be free
Live now,
Give hope
Show how.
Share love
Take care,
Stand tall
Play fair.
Know right
From wrong,
Be happy
Live long.

Unlimited... Mysterious...
Powerful... Sublime...
Are the least that you are
In Space and Time.

The stars all shine
With a story to tell,
And the moon, it knows,
Where the mystery dwells:
On an emerald planet
Suspended in space,
Where your dreams come true
When you act with faith!

Cast yesterday aside,
And bid tomorrow adieu,
Because there's nothing
Here and Now
That you can't do.

It's not the score
That makes us great,
Nor is it the wealth
We strive to create.
But that we live our lives
In pursuit of the truth,
And honor the dreams
We dreamt in our youth.

Warning!
Thoughts become things...
Choose them wisely.

A life is not measured
By the games that are won,
But that you lived in the moment
And learned how to have fun.

Two hearts that beat
Like yours and mine,
Will love beyond
The end of time.

Over the moon
And past the stars,
When you dream with a friend
You fly twice as far!

There are only miracles.

Your angels are there
In your time of need,
Not to question or judge
But to give you a lead.
It may be a vision
Or a voice you hear,
They just want to show you
That magic is near.
So pick yourself up
And go after your dream,
You could never have
A better home team!

I'm through with pleasing everyone,
I'm done with fooling me,
It's time I started living life,
The way I want it to be!

If all of the people
In all of the world
Could turn their worries into laughter,
Then all of the people
In all of the world
Would live happily ever after.

To dwell upon what might have been,
Is, perhaps, the greatest sin.

To want,
To need,
To dream
And grow,
Reveals the secrets
We came here to know.

Time and Space
Aren't quite as they seem,
Just magical props
In a magical dream.

Like the sound of waves
Crashing onto the beach,
Or the call of a gull
To those out of reach.
There are wonders hidden
In the world around you,
And each time you find one
You're given a clue-
To the magic of life
And the mystery it keeps,
Where never a dream
Lies outside of your reach.

Let me walk
With my own self,
In a wondrous, glorious dream.
And down this path
That we shall tread,
We'll be an invincible team.

<u>Your Angel</u>
Since the dawn of time
We've been one in the same,
And your smile and laughter
Have been my sole aim.
So never forget
When the chips are down,
I'm busy at work
To turn things around!

Live, laugh, love, and have fun...
Just a moment more,
And your turn will be done.

If I had only known
Just how well I'd really do,
The journey would have mattered
Instead, alas, it's through.
And don't you really know it,
That in the end you'll say,
I'd trade this pot of gold
For just another single day.

It's not the score
Nor how often you win,
But that you face the fears
That lurk within.

October 31

When the sun descends
And the owls take flight,
Sounds from the past
Soon fill the night.
So beware my friend
When you leave your home,
On Halloween night
You won't be alone!

As many fish as there are in the sea,
There's none I'd rather be than me!

Do not look down upon another
Nor judge the days they keep,
Your thoughts can wound like daggers
And cause the sky to weep.
Each one of us is special
With a mystery all our own,
And left to walk our own path
We'll sooner make it home.

In the depths of space,
There isn't a trace,
Of the power that
Brought it to be.
But it cannot hide
If you look "inside",
It was the Spirit Of Life
Set free.

Cast your fears
Into the sea,
Life needs you dear...
Entirely.

Visualize a planet
Where all creatures are one,
And happiness will flower
Brighter than the sun.

Born of imagination
Your thoughts are things,
With magical powers
That know how to bring:
Your dreams to life
And your nightmares too,
So watch what you think
Or it could happen to you!

The sun and the moon
Keep watch from above,
And light our way
With infinite love.

What has passed, has passed,
And matters no more-
Looking back in life
doesn't better the score.

You can travel the earth
Far and wide,
But from my love
You can never hide.

Abundance is your birthright
And your thoughts unlock the doors,
Just know that you deserve it
And act as if it is yours.
There's enough to go around,
Much more than you might think,
And the Universe is yearning
To fill you to the brink.

If you see it, touch it.
If you touch it, feel it.
If you feel it, love it.
If you love it,
Give it.

A dream's just a dream,
Until you can see,
Yourself in the picture —
Like it was meant to be.

Money is power
It'll put shoes on your feet,
But that power is limited
By the time that you keep.
You can charge by the hour
Or the seeds that you sow,
It makes little difference
If you really want to know.
Because the mark of achievement
For your time in the sun,
Is the love that you shared
Before your life was done.

In this journey called life
I know in my heart,
That be it ever so humble
I'm glad for my part.

Be true to yourself
In the games that you play,
Or it could be your dreams
That you one day betray.

I am the bird in flight
And the sky it seeks,
I am the sun at dawn
Rising over the peaks.
I am the voice you hear
When the clouds turn gray,
And the hand you hold
When you've lost your way.
And though you forget me
From time to time,
Even now I am with you...
As you read this rhyme.

You are never alone.

It's really quite simple,
You just have to believe-
That life is for living
All the dreams you conceive.

To be or not to be,
Depends on what you do,
For actions speak louder than words,
But to act is up to you.

All of time will wait for you
As the night enfolds the day,
But if you really want to get things done
You had better seize the day!

All knowledge is yours
But you must seek it first,
If you want the answers
That will quench your thirst.
And though the hunt may be long
It is from the quest,
That you'll quiet the hunger
And give your soul rest.
But the search is doomed
From the very start,
If you look for life's answers
Outside of your heart.

Move through all your doubts,
And get past all your tears,
For paradise is lingering
Just beyond all your fears.

Every dream you dream
Will one day come true,
So dream your dreams-
   All they need is you!

Everything's gonna...B.O.K.

Can't get it?
Don't sweat it,
Let it come to you!
If it's right,
And you hold tight,
Your dreams will all come true!

Seek your gold
But don't look too far,
Or the life you lead
Could fade like a star.
Open your heart
And look within,
For the joys of life
Reside therein.

The world is your oyster
And life is your ocean,
Just follow your heart
To set the waves in motion!

If every flower
Tried to look like another,
They'd forget that they're special
And unlike any other.

Would, that I could,
Give the answers in time,
But the truth that you seek
Is different than mine.

Take your time
And worry no more,
Rushing around
Won't settle the score.
The voice within
Knows what you should do,
Just listen to it
And follow through.

The call of a whale
To those out of reach,
Echoes a secret
They long to teach:
That material things
Quickly sink out of view,
But time shared with a friend
Is forever with you.

A dolphin smiles
Because it's happy to be,
Alive in a world
Where the best things are free!

The depths of the ocean
Will never compare,
To the rift of a heart
In need of repair.
Seems the pain grows stronger
With each passing beat,
To the point of conceding
Your whole life in defeat.
But you're not so lucky,
As it continues in vain,
Pounding like thunder
In a driving rain.
Yet as the storm slowly lifts
You see a small light,
That beckons you further
And eases your plight.
It begins to enfold you
As your heart starts to mend,
With the long lost memory
That you're your own best friend.

If all the "WANT"
Were squelched in me,
There'd be no march
Through eternity.

A celebration of stars
Dance into the night,
One for each dream
About to take flight.
And by dawn's early hour
They all have a plan:
To burst into your life
As fast as they can.
But you've got to believe,
That dreams really come true,
If you want all the gifts
That are waiting for you!

I am you,
And you are me.
All is one,
And will always be.

The magic in life
Is far too great,
To spend your time
Waiting on fate.
In just a blink
Your dreams are born,
And when you act with faith
They begin to take form.

Imagination...is everything.

When you think a brand new thought
Something comes alive,
And when you think this
Brand new thought
It will strive, and strive, and strive,
To find its place
In Time and Space,
To reach the light of day—
So think your new thought all the time,
To help it find its way!

The secret of life
Is not to resist,
But to ride the tide
In search of your bliss.

Hey, little girl
Did you know as you sleep,
I'm out in the fields
Growing barley and wheat.
And you little boy
As you play in the sand,
I'm working all day
As hard as I can.
So that when you both grow-up
And leave Mommy and me,
You'll be proud of the man
I tried to be.

I've started a journey
I'll see through to the end,
And I'm ever so grateful
It includes you,
My friend.

Some presents are big
Some presents are small,
But those from the heart
Are the best presents of all!

When you
Are you,
You are
Unique.

Your name was whispered
Before you were born,
And out from the mist
Your image took form.
The Spirit of Life
Had begun its quest,
To know of itself
Through the ultimate test:
A Being of Light
Set free in creation,
To master the gift
Of imagination!

Mind over matter,
And limitations shatter.

Talk a little, sing a lot,
Walk a little, dance a lot,
Smile a little, laugh a lot,
Dream a little, live a lot.

Our paths have crossed
On our way back home,
Making small the price
Of ever being alone.

The forest is hushed
With still fallen snow,
As the moon casts light
On the earth below.
There isn't a soul
On the planet this night,
Not bathed in a love
From a distant site.
It's Christmas eve
And throughout the land,
Every living thing lies
In the palm of one hand.

Dream on and dream big,
They're all meant to be,
Just imagine them done
And they're history.

Think it, talk it,
Live it, show it.
Whatever you want,
Let the Universe know it!

Dinosaur's Lament

I'm one of the creatures
Who used to live here,
The earth was my playground
And I loved it dear.
I thought it was mine
And I thought it would last,
But now as you know
I'm a thing of the past.
So be careful you humans
Or soon you may see,
How easy it is
To become history!

You're the kind of person
That's hard to forget,
A one-in-a-million
To the people you've met.
Your friends are as varied
As the places you go,
And they all want to tell you
In case you don't know:
That you make a big difference
In the lives that you touch,
By taking so little
And giving so much!

It's you who decides
On your mission and fate,
For how else could you learn
Of your gift to create?

M-agically
I-ncited
R-eality
A-djustment
C-oncealed by
L-oving
E-ntities

I am a thought,
I make dreams come true.
But that's just the half
Of what we thoughts can do.
Please use great care,
When you choose what you think,
Cause whatever it is,
Might appear in a blink.
That's what we do,
In time and in space,
As soon as we're thought,
We look for our place.
For better or worse,
To win or to lose,
The thing to remember,
Is that you get to choose.

Blessed are emotions
For though some make you weep,
You're better to have known them
For the secrets that they keep.

The mysteries of your soul begin,
To show themselves when you look within.

There's an essence among us
Sent here from above,
And it longs to embrace us
With infinite love.
But to feel this great gift
You have to know from the start–
No matter how far you've strayed
You're still in God's heart.

It's the little things you do
That make the big things happen!

Escape the ordinary,
Run for your life,
Let go of your fears,
And let your dreams take flight!

To most I'm a face
Lost in the race,
But really...
I've already won!

The Lighthouse

Caught between swells and lost in the night,
The captain and crew
Quickly vanished from sight.
The ship's lurching bow had shuddered in pain,
And her sails were like ribbons
Cut through by the rain.
And then, without warning,
As all hope gave out,
A mate still on deck let out with a shout:
"To the God Of The Sea,
And the Lord Of The Night,
It may be our death, but first we must fight!"
Then as crew sprang to life
No longer fearing their plight,
They beheld in the distance
A shimmering light...
A moment had passed
Before their cries turned to laughter -
You're never lost in this life
When you know what you're after!

To be all you can be,
To give all you can give,
To love all you can love,
And to live all you can live...
Just ask.

Whatever you want,
Wants you!

Let there be magic
In all that you do,
It's part of the promise
That life made to you.

Thoughts are the things
That draw life to you,
Like a magnet to steel
They're how dreams come true.
It's really that easy
And a whole lot of fun,
Just know what you want
And imagine it done!

You yearn
You go,
You learn
You grow.

Roses are red
Violets are blue,
If the earth dies
So will you!

I'm beginning to see,
Though not with my eyes,
That the magic of life
Lies deaf to our cries.
Alone we have chosen
Our time and our space,
To get on with our lessons
And have fun in this place.
To win or to lose
Is not why we've come,
But to live through the journey
Until it is done.

The stars all know
What we're about to discover,
That all mankind
Must love one another.

I AM...anything I choose to be!

There are times when you stumble
And there are times when you're lost,
But to get where you're going,
These are well worth their cost.

Let your burning *desire*
Set the world on fire!

Once upon a time
There was a place called earth,
Where Mother Nature and
Man lived as one.
But a revolution began
And man forgot where he had come from.
Money, lust, greed and hate
Took over man's fate,
But it wasn't too late.
Man learned to recycle,
Turn off lights, carpool,
And buy environmentally safe products.
Man and earth lived happily ever after.

Beneath the waves
Where time stands still,
All creatures know
From fin to gill:
That gold be rare
And too precious to lend,
But the greatest treasure
Is to have a best friend.

A lot of time I wasted,
Wishing I could be,
The opposite of everything
My mirror showed to me.
But then one day I realized,
The only thing to do,
Was try to be a better me
And not another you.

What's the hurry,
The world will wait,
There's no need to rush
Before heaven's gate.

I'm history in the making
And I want the world to know,
Whether you think I'm a fool or a hero
You're in for one heck of a show!

The miracle of the ocean
Is the same in you and me:
Whatever it is we think on
Will soon come to be.
Imagination is the force
That turns our lives around,
Like the currents underwater
It moves without a sound.
Believe that you can do it
And know you have the powers,
Then all your dreams will come to pass
As the waves unfold the hours.

Be bold and go forth
Like it was meant to be,
Your dreams are the gifts
That will set you free.

You're one in billion,
My love till the end,
Too bad you're just a tree
My tall and shady friend.

Go north and dance with the polar bears,
Go south and laugh with the penguins,
Go west and fish, go east and wish
For planet earth.

What once was a dream
Has now come to pass,
As the stone and the clay
Were first ether and gas.
And so it has been
Within time and space,
Where all of your thoughts
Yearn for their place.
They are sent to earth
On the day they're conceived,
And are brought to life
Once you really believe!

The deep blue sea spoke to me,
It was holding back a mystery.
A dolphin took me by the hand,
It wanted me to understand:
That in this life there's more to behold,
Than bags of money and pots of gold.
Believe in yourself and you will see,
How happy and free
You were meant to be!

This book has now been printed, and reprinted many times. At the time of this printing, our T-shirt business is run from www.andydooley.com. Sheelagh is writing future best sellers and screenplays. And Mike has founded TUT's Adventurers Club, for the adventure of life, with members in over 72 countries. To become an Adventurer and to begin receiving Mike's daily inspirational "Notes from the Universe" emailings, absolutely FREE, just take the Oath at:

www.tut.com

Other TUT Publications available at
www.tut.com, or bookstores everywhere:

Dandelion,
The Extraordinary Life of a Misfit
Paperback, Sheelagh Mawe, 1994

Lost in Space
Paperback, Mike Dooley, 1998

Thoughts Become Things * LIVE!
Audio tape/CD, Mike Dooley, 2001

Infinite Possibilities:
The Art of Living Your Dreams
Audio Program, Mike Dooley, 2002

Notes from the Universe
Screensaver Software, Mike Dooley, 2002

Notes from the Universe
Hardcover, Mike Dooley, 2003

Totally Unique Thoughts®
...because thoughts become things!®

TUT believes that everyone is special, that every life is meaningful, and that we're all here to learn that dreams really do come true.

We also believe that "thoughts become things" and that imagination is the gift that can bring love, health, abundance and happiness into our lives.

Totally Unique Thoughts®
TUT® Enterprises, Inc.
Orlando, Florida
www.tut.com
U.S.A.

Michael and Andrew Dooley, with their mother Sheelagh Mawe, co-founded TUT in 1989. Today Sheelagh is a full-time author (Dandelion, TUT '94; Grown Men, Avon '97) and Mike and Andy continue to live, love and learn at "TUT World Headquarters" in Orlando, Florida.
Photo circa 1995.